Dear Mom,

    I remember recently looking back through some old photographs and being struck by what a lovely girl you were. What a catch you must have been for my dad! It seems I'm still being struck by your enjoyment and experience of life, even as I find out things I never knew about you.

Dear Mom,

I remember recently
looking back through
some old photographs
and being drawn to
what I loved. What a
... that have been for me
dad! It seems
still being drawn to
your enjoyment and
experiences of life, even as
I find out more right
now there when you

"Like roses, children thrive on love."

A tribute to my mother:

_____
_____
_____
_____
_____
_____
_____
_____
_____
_____
_____
_____
_____
_____
_____
_____
_____
_____
_____
_____

A TRIBUTE TO MOTHERS

Heartstrings

OF LAUGHTER & LOVE

COUNTRYMAN

Special thanks to all who wrote tributes to their mothers
and to everyone who contributed hands
and hearts to produce this book.

Grateful acknowledgement is made to the following publishers
and copyright holders for permission to reprint copyrighted material:

Emilie Barnes. *If Teacups Could Talk*. Eugene, Ore.: Harvest House, 1994.
Charles Colson. *A Dance with Deception*. Dallas: Word, 1993.
Ruth Bell Graham. *Sitting by My Laughing Fire*. Dallas: Word, 1977.
Phillip Keller. *Wonder O' the Wind*. Dallas: Word, 1982.
Edna Lewis. *A Taste of Country Cooking*. New York: Alfred A. Knopf, 1976.
Dennis Rainey. *The Tribute*. Nashville: Thomas Nelson, 1994.
Charles Swindoll. *The Finishing Touch*. Dallas: Word, 1994.

Notice: Every effort has been made to locate the copyright owners
of the material used in this book. Please let us know if an error has been made,
and we will make any necessary changes in subsequent printings.

J. Countryman is a trademark of Thomas Nelson, Inc.

A J. Countryman Book
Designed by Left Coast Design, Portland, Oregon
Compiled and edited by Terri Gibbs
Cover photo by Michelle Clement

ISBN: 0-8499-5492-4

Printed in Hong Kong

This book is a present to mothers, a tribute of honor for the unique qualities and goodness that each pours into the life of her child. When I think of the essence of my mother's life, I remember the winter of my sixth year.

Dad was going to college and, with four school-age children to feed, money was scarce. Dreading the thought of four empty stockings on Christmas morning, Dad decided he would get a job at night to earn extra money. Mom knew this would cut into his precious study time just when final papers and exams were approaching, so she suggested an alternate plan— she would try selling her sweet rolls.

For the next several weeks, while we were at school each day, she made dozens of wonderful sweet rolls, smothered in a creamy, white sugar-glaze with nuts and cherry and pineapple fillings oozing over the sides. As soon as we got home from school she would hand us packages of warm rolls wrapped in foil to sell to the neighbors. It was terribly cold so we tucked the rolls into our coats to keep warm. I was afraid to go up to the doors at first, but when the neighbors began praising the delectable sweet rolls and buying all our packages with orders for more, my courage increased. Soon I was striding happily up and down the campus streets, proud to be selling my mother's confections—proud that we were helping my father earn high marks on his studies.

This little incident is a cameo of my mother's life—one of resourcefulness, determination, and a deep, abiding love for her family. She has always been happiest when giving and doing for others. What a great treasure that this mother should be mine!

This book is dedicated to all beloved mothers. It is a collection—gifts of gratitude to our mothers for the love we can never truly repay.

May God bless and reward our dear mothers,
both here on earth and in heaven.

Terri Gibbs
EDITOR

I know of no more permanent imprint on a life than the one made by mothers.

CHARLES SWINDOLL

Dear Mom,

What I really want to tell you, Mom, is that I count it a privilege and blessing to be able to take care of your needs. I will never be able to repay you for the care, love, and sacrifice you have given to me over the years. Please don't ever feel bad about asking for my help.

You are a special lady. Your life has been good but not easy. I look back to when Dad died and only now as an adult do I realize exactly what you went through then. Three kids to raise and no financial help. God was faithful and we never did without. I praise you for your strength and character that kept you going on our behalf.

I love you,

BETTY DILLON

The most glorious sight that one ever sees beneath
the stars is the sight of worthy motherhood.

GEORGE W. TRUETT

My mother used to look out the window every morning
and say, "Maybe this will be the day when Christ comes again."
She lived with that daily anticipation. . . . It was my mother's
hope until she went at last to be with him. . . .

Billy Graham

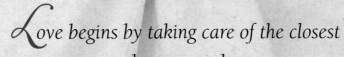

Love begins by taking care of the closest ones—the ones at home.

MOTHER TERESA

Dear Mother,

Thank you for the example you have been to me. You may be only 4 feet 7 inches tall, but in my eyes you have always stood tall.

From my early childhood I can remember how our home was always open to anyone and everyone who needed food, fellowship, or fun! We played many silly games with anyone who expressed the slightest interest. I remember how you would fix homemade cream puffs every Friday night for all the kids in the neighborhood. No wonder the kids all loved to come to our house!

I recall those years in Alaska when we would move all of our furniture to set up tables for holiday meals so all the military boys and families who were away from relatives could come to our home.

In sixty-one years of marriage and ministry, you and Daddy have given of yourselves unselfishly. At times I wonder how you've been able to do so much all these years . . . surely it is through God's grace. Only eternity will reveal the lives you have touched by the love you have always shown to others. Your example has taught me to love others also. I am so grateful that you are my mother!

MARY M.

The process of shaping the child . . . shapes
also the mother herself. Reverence for her sacred burden
calls her to all that is pure and good, that she may teach
primarily by her own humble, daily example.

Elisabeth Elliot

THE SHAPING OF A CHRISTIAN FAMILY

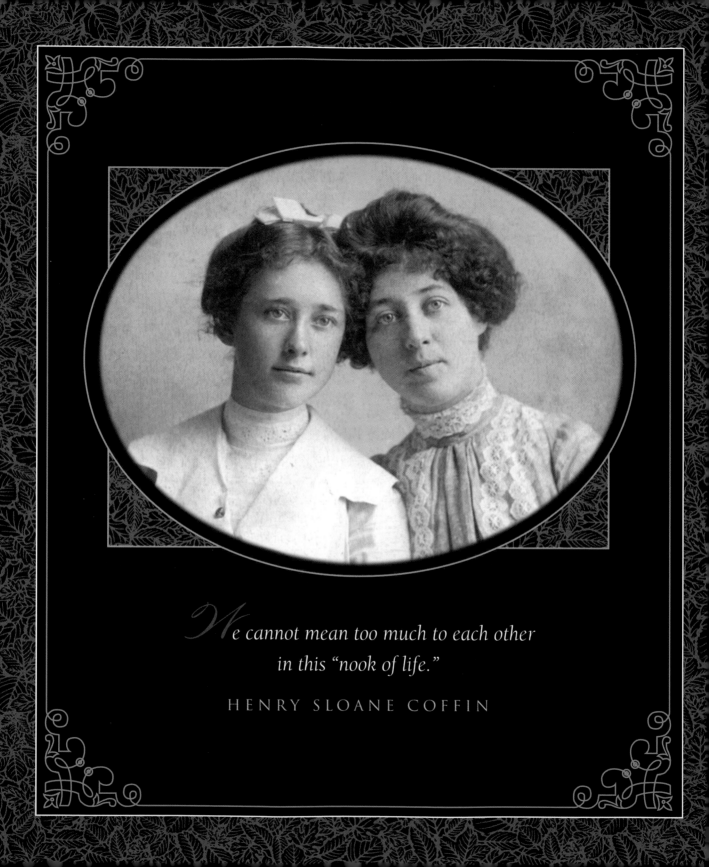

*We cannot mean too much to each other
in this "nook of life."*

HENRY SLOANE COFFIN

Dear Mother,

I learned much about God through your example—His love, patience, and tender heart were clearly demonstrated in your life. Thank you for the time we spent making ice cream out of snow during that cold winter.

Wonderful \wən-dər-fəl\ adj. 1: exciting wonder: marvelous, astonishing. 2: unusually good: admirable. SEE ALSO: MY MOTHER.

A. PAUL MYERS

A mother keeps a vigil at the bedside of her sick child.
The world calls it "fatigue" but she calls it love.

FULTON J. SHEEN

My father's salary was very small, so there were
economies of every kind. Mother had learned to sew by a
Singer Sewing Machine company correspondence course, and she
did ingenious things with fabric bought on sale—remnants— . . . Her
cooking of necessity had to be simple, but she gave things a twist as to
flavor and beauty. When I wanted to earn money by starting a candy
business, many long hours she helped me to make fudge and penuche
and coconut bars, until she got neuritis in her shoulder from doing
so much hand beating. We made the magnificent sum
of seventy dollars from our combined efforts.

Edith Schaeffer
THE TAPESTRY

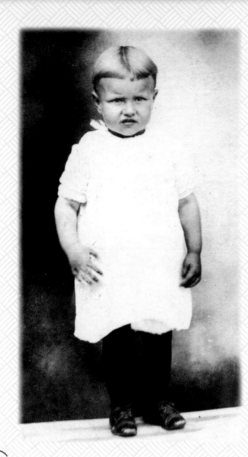

$\mathcal{A}$ll that is purest and best in man
is but the echo of a mother's benediction.

FREDERICK W. MORTON

Dear Mom,

$\mathcal{Y}$ou have a love that is all-encompassing, never fading, ever-expanding
— your devotion and tenderness are the closest thing I know to the infinite
love of God.

LUKE G.

A Mother's Prayer

What wears me out
are little things:
angels minus
shining wings.
Forgive me, Lord,
if I have whined;
. . . it takes so much
to keep them shined;
yet each small rub
has its reward,
for they have blessed *me*.

Thank you,
Lord.

Ruth Bell Graham

SITTING BY MY LAUGHING FIRE

*D*uty makes us do things well, but love makes us do them beautifully.

PHILLIPS BROOKS

A mother is completely fatigued. She has been telling her friends
for weeks that there is nothing left of her, and then a child falls ill
and needs her. Week after week, by night and day, she stands
by and never thinks of being tired.

HARRY EMERSON FOSDICK

"*Lying there after her ordeal, with the baby on her arm, she knew the age-old surge of mother-love. All her old love of life seemed to concentrate on one thing—the little soft, helpless bundle.*"

BESS STREETER ALDRICH

"A LANTERN IN HER HAND"

Dear Mom,

Remember when I was only three and you opened the screen door for me and secured me in your long, cotton apron? I was SO afraid of that old tramp! And later when I felt God's call to go to Africa as a missionary—so far away—you never let me doubt it or disobey God. You kept praying for me and every week I knew I could read another of your newsy letters. One day you told me, "I always knew you were a winner."

I can still see you as I walked into that hospital room late one Sunday. You exclaimed, "Oh, you have come!" . . . and the smile, you were so happy. Thanks, Mom, for these happy memories.

MARJORIE M.

To feel loved, to belong, to have a place,
and to hear one's dignity and worth often affirmed—
these are to the soul what food is to the body.

ANNE ORTLUND

My mother, whose disposition was always bright and optimistic,
was active, energetic and wholly devoted to her large family. No sacrifice
was too great, no task too hard, for her willing heart and hands. Her
work was hard and her hours long. Only God knows the number
of nights she walked the floor, rocked the cradle, or sat by the
bedside of her children during their many, many ailments.

Oswald J. Smith
THE STORY OF MY LIFE

Canning Time

"In late summer, my mama would begin canning in earnest. Sometimes her sisters would come from the city to help, and they would bring their children along. These visits were the only vacations my city cousins ever had. . . .

What happy days. Canning time wasn't just work for my mama and aunts; it was also a social event, almost like a quilting bee. For us children, it was even better than the county fair."

DORI SANDERS
COUNTRY COOKING

GREEN BEAN SALAD WITH VINAIGRETTE

For the dressing combine:

2 garlic cloves, crushed • 2 teaspoons grated onion
2 tablespoon Dijon mustard • 1 cup olive oil
1/2 cup rice wine vinegar
1 teaspoon fresh, crushed black pepper
1 teaspoon kosher salt • 1/2 cup chopped fresh parsley
1 1/2 teaspoons thyme • 1 1/2 teaspoons rosemary

For the salad prepare:

2 pounds fresh green beans, ends removed
2 yellow or red bell peppers, julienned

Place the green beans in a large steam pot and sprinkle with kosher salt. Steam until just crunchy and still bright green. Rinse in cold water to stop the cooking. Drain and set aside.

Put the beans and bell peppers in a large bowl and toss with the dressing. Let the mixture sit for a half hour and serve. Top with freshly grated Parmesan cheese. Serves 6.

T.G.

$\mathscr{S}$lipping on Mother's old apron is like getting a big hug from her.

JOYCE SMITH

$\mathscr{I}$n my childhood home, we would spend an hour at the table after we had eaten, talking or reading Bible story books. I don't recall the little ones fussing. Mother would hold the baby and Father would hold the next and I'd hold the next. There was real togetherness.

Ingrid Trobisch

My earliest childhood memories
include sitting at [my mother's] feet in various
study groups as she quarried the books
of Ezekiel, Daniel, and Revelation for
their wealth of insights about the
future which God had in store
for Israel and the church.

David Allan
Hubbard

Dear Mother,

You are ninety years of age! You have given birth to nine children. During the span of years that we were all home, we were under the tutelage of your watchful eye. You and Dad reared us to be God-fearing, law-abiding, and respectful of others. During these sunset years, we nine children just want you to know that you are always in our thoughts, our hearts, and our prayers.

Love,

GEORGE S.

Judicious mothers will always keep in mind that they are the first book read, and the last put aside in every child's library.

C. LENOX REDMOND

When driving in the family carriage from Blairbeth to Glasgow, Mother would frequently see a pale face pressed against the window high up in one of the tenements. One day she had the coachman stop the carriage and, alighting, made her way through the "close" and up the dark winding stairway to the chamber where she had seen the face at the window. There she found a frail, crippled girl. After that visit Mother started a Friday-night Bible class for mill girls. . . . Yes, Mother, thou hast reaped well indeed. . . . Not empty-handed didst thou go to the King's Gate.

Clarence Macarthey
THE MAKING OF A MINISTER

"Under the elm-tree stood a pretty tea table, covered with bread and butter, custards and berries, and in the middle a fine cake with sugar-roses on the top; and mamma and baby, all nicely dressed, were waiting to welcome them to the birthday feast."

LOUISA MAY ALCOTT

"SHADOW CHILDREN"

Women like to make sacrifices in one big piece, to give God something grand, but we can't. Our lives are a mosaic of little things, like putting a rose in a vase on the table.

INGRID TROBISCH

Dear Momma,

How can I thank you for all you taught me? Your love of life, music, and family will always be interwoven into my person. I will never forget the hundreds of times you played the piano while Sissy and I danced our own terrible ballet.

Now that you are gone, I realize the music of your life still plays in my life—and that it doesn't matter how I dance, just as long as I do.

Your daughter,

JANA M.

Home is meant to be a place where human relationships are to be understood for all the situations in later life, and where a shelter is to be found for all sorts of hurts, physical and emotional.

Edith Schaeffer

God could not be everywhere, and therefore He made mothers.

JEWISH PROVERB

A Tribute to Our Beloved Mum,
Myrtle Ivy McMartin,
from Her Daughters

Our mother's life drew together so many Christlike characteristics that the Bible praises and the world desperately needs. Always manifesting unruffled strength and gentleness, her love for God and her faith in God were unshakable. Mum trusted God for each one of her children. She prayed for us, believed in us, and loved all of us unconditionally. We are fulfilling our God-given destinies because our mother dedicated her life to bringing us up in the way of the Lord. As a grandma she somehow planted herself forever in each grandchild's young heart. She has finished her time here on earth, but her influence keeps flowing on down through her children and her grandchildren. One can only imagine the beauty of our mum as she worships around the eternal throne.

We love you Mum,

JEAN, LYNNE, AND RUTH

(New South Wales, Australia)

. . . A woman who fears the LORD, she shall be praised.

PROVERBS 31:30

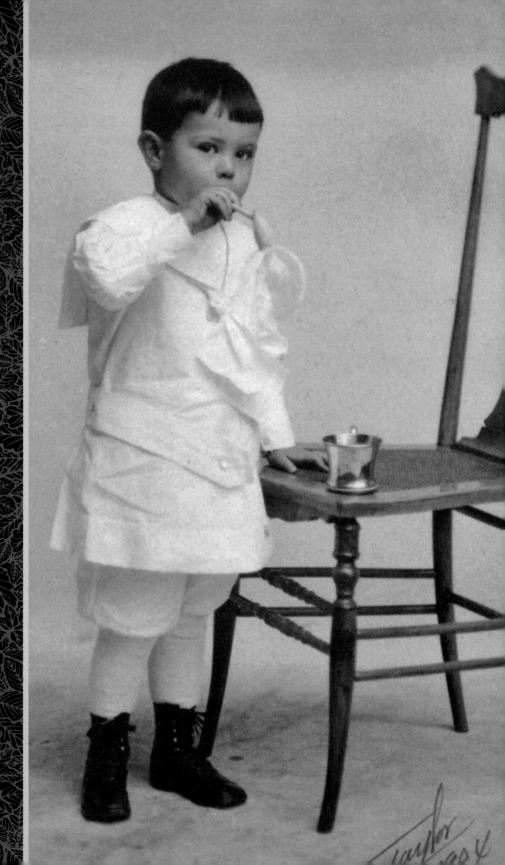

> *No man is poor who had a godly mother.*
>
> ABRAHAM
> LINCOLN

(*The Tribute*, by Dennis Rainey)

Dear Mom,

I remember recently looking back through some old photographs and being struck by what a lovely girl you were. What a catch you must have been for my dad! It seems I'm still being struck by your enjoyment and experience of life, even as I find out things I never knew about you. Why is it you never told me that you and your best girlfriend jumped off a moving train together?

The farther I go in life the more grateful I am that you are my mother. You've poured so much of your life into me. . . . As a grown-up, now I can see you in a different light. I understand some of the sacrifices you made in order to nurture me. I thank you for caring about my self-esteem. I know there were times when I disappointed you and even broke your heart, but you never stopped loving me. . . . I will always love you, Mother.

Your beloved son,

DAVID MCKNIGHT

When I was a boy, my mother and I would make eye contact, and she would give me a smile that would make my day. Her eyes and her smile would say, "I love you, you're terrific." She was the center of my universe, and, like most children, I thought I had the most wonderful mother in the world. I adored her.

BOB KEESHAN
(CAPTAIN KANGAROO)

My earliest memories are of wobbling down the stairs and seeing my mom at the kitchen table with her Bible and her coffee, spending time with the Lord. That scene was always a source of great comfort and stability for me.

Steve Green

*M*other did not think of herself as deeply spiritual. She would have protested if anyone had said she was. But she was certainly hungry for God, deeply conscious of her own weakness and need of Him. Called to be a mother, entrusted with the holy task of cooperating with God in shaping the destinies of six people, she knew it was too heavy a burden to carry alone. She did not try. She went to Him whose name is Wonderful Counsellor, Mighty God, Everlasting Father. She asked His help—daily.

Elisabeth Elliot

THE SHAPING OF A CHRISTIAN FAMILY

*P*arents who care unselfishly for their children, who provide for them spiritually as well as materially, are performing an invaluable service. They are helping to create a stable and secure world.

ROBERT MCCRACKEN

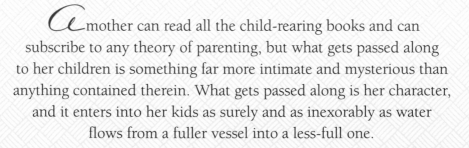

A mother can read all the child-rearing books and can subscribe to any theory of parenting, but what gets passed along to her children is something far more intimate and mysterious than anything contained therein. What gets passed along is her character, and it enters into her kids as surely and as inexorably as water flows from a fuller vessel into a less-full one.

LAURENCE SHAMES

"The nursery was a big room, and in the evening a bright wood-fire always burned there for baby. Mamma sat before it softly rubbing baby's little rosy limbs before she went to bed, singing and telling stories meanwhile to the three children who pranced about in their long nightgowns."

LOUISA MAY ALCOTT
"SHADOW CHILDREN"

I am not in any doubt as to how my own Christian experience began. The altar before which I knelt first was my mother's knee.

L. D. WEATHERHEAD

She Was My Mother!

She was brave! And she was beautiful!

*M*y earliest recollections of her were of a wondrous woman of warmth, vibrancy, and overflowing good cheer. Despite the depravity and degradation of the African tribespeople among whom she lived and worked with such goodwill, there emanated from her an enormous enthusiasm for life. . . .

Her complexion was almost flawless. Despite the dryness of the desperate African sun; despite the ravages of tropical disease—her face glowed with a radiance of remarkable joy. Her ready smile, her happy humor, her vibrant voice had won her the admiration of others who often called her "Sister Sunshine."

Yet her humble home was a typical African frontier house built of crooked, hand-cut poles, plastered with mud, coated with cow dung, . . . and thatched with grass.

For her, life—all of life—was a great adventure with God. He and she were constant companions in an unfolding drama of divine design. Nothing that happened in her adventuresome and exciting career was ever an accident. Of this she was sure. . . .

A certain wondrous wholesomeness marked her life and conduct. She was born to be brave. She was bound to be beautiful. . . . With joy and gracious generosity she was glad to give and give and give of herself to enrich others. . . .

Again and again in later years I was to see her storm into native villages to rescue women and children abused and beaten by their drunken husbands and fathers. She was a lovely lady with the heart of a lion. In utter, raw, selflessness she would gladly, heroically lay down her life for the sake of others.

She was my mother! . . . How favored was I to have been mothered by such a wondrous woman of incandescent faith in God.

W. Phillip Keller
WONDER O' THE WIND

Dear Jody (my birthmother):

Thank you will never be enough to express my heartfelt gratitude. Thank you for taking the difficult high road. Thank you for sharing me with parents who could not bear their own children.
Thank you for putting
    my life,
       my comfort,
          my future,
            my well-being
ahead of your own.

I carry your gift of courage and selflessness with me always.

          With love,

PAMELA M.

Dear Mom,

Remember the art project I brought home to you as a gift one year in grade school? It was a bright yellow, clay pancake—my own creation—with a childlike "21" carved into the center. I remember how surprised and pleased you were when I explained that the numbers represented your age . . . I had underestimated by about a decade.

You still haven't aged in my eyes. Your body may grow older and more tired, but you are always young to me.

          Always your girl,

PAMELA M.

Many women have done excellently, but you surpass them all.

PROVERBS 31:29

To Mother

You painted no Madonnas
On chapel walls in Rome,
But with a touch diviner
You lived one in your home. . . .

You built no great cathedrals
That centuries applaud
But with a grace exquisite
Your life cathedraled God. . . .

T. W. FESSENDEN

My mother was a striking beauty who left the world
a more beautiful place than she found it. She grew lovely flowers,
did the finest needlepoint I have ever seen, and knew
how to keep an exquisite home. . . .

She taught me a great deal, although neither of us realized it at
the time. Probably her most important lesson was an inadvertent one.
You have two choices in life: You can like what you do, or
you can dislike it. I have chosen to like it.

Barbara Bush

A MEMOIR

When I was just eleven, after my alcoholic father died, my mother moved us into those three little rooms behind her little dress shop. Mama had to work long hours to provide for my brother and me. She designed and sold dresses, took care of alterations, and often worked far into the night doing the books. . . .

And yet, in spite of it all, Mama always managed to have time for a tea party. She would invite a guest—a friend or a neighbor or a customer—through the little curtain that served as our front door. Then it would be time to put on the kettle, warm up the teapot, look for some cookies, and carefully lift the cups from their place of honor in the cabinet. Before I knew it, we would be having a party.

Emilie Barnes

IF TEACUPS COULD TALK

*Nobility of character is the most precious heritage
of a family, and it is transmitted from generation to generation
by personal association and inspiration.*

ROBERT McCRACKEN

*There is a saying that as you become older you find yourself
turning into your parents. If this is true, I take comfort in the fact that
perhaps I will one day be like my mother—a constant loving presence
in the lives of my children as they grow and have children of their own.
As a child, I took motherhood (and my mother) for granted; however,
now that I have a child and family of my own, I understand the
responsibilities, joys, and sacrifices of motherhood in an entirely
new perspective. I am grateful to my mother for her willingness
to put her family first and to sacrifice her own needs for ours.
While our love may have failed or disappointed her at times,
her love and support for us never faltered or wavered.*

KATHRYN M.

*There is no higher height to which humanity
can attain than that occupied by a converted,
heaven-inspired, praying mother.*

ANONYMOUS

. . . Once again, mother's very real bank account had provided the necessary provision at a time of need. From those hours spent alone with God each day had come her supreme confidence that He would provide out of His limitless supply. . . .

Out of this solid wealth, this certainty, Mother could always afford to give to others, not just material things, but showering sparks of imagination, a gleam of hope, a thrust of courage—qualities that contained more substance than the coin of any realm and which opened the door for fulfillment in many a life she touched.

Catherine Marshall
A CLOSER WALK

❧

A home is a kingdom of its own in the midst of the world, a stronghold amid life's storms and stresses, a refuge, even a sanctuary.

DIETRICH BONHOEFFER

❧

Tradition is not just what we receive, it is what we create with our own hands and then hand over, the ties we make with past and future.

MARCIA FALK

Dear Louy [Louisa May Alcott],

I am glad you put your heart in the right place;
for I am sure all true strength comes from above.
Continue to feel that God is near you, dear child, and
He never will forsake you in a weak moment. Write
me always when you feel that I can help you; for, though God
is near, Mother never forgets you, and your refuge is her arms. . . .

Mother

LOUISA MAY ALCOTT: LIFE, LETTERS, AND JOURNALS

$\mathcal{A}$ mother's days are made wearisome by the wants and
frequent waywardness of little children, and her nights are often made
wakeful by their illnesses. But while those little ones are burdens,
they are such lovable bundles of graceful curves and such
constant sources of surprise and joy.

RALPH SOCKMAN

I made it a rule to take my children one at a time into my room; and having been careful to see that they were comfortably seated . . . I would say, "I'm going to talk to Jesus," and then before my child, would pour out my soul to Him. Oh, how precious are the memories of little pinafores lifted to wipe my eyes or the sound of sweet little voices saying, "Don't cry, Mother."

AMELIA HUDSON BROOMHALL

1875

*B*eautiful faces are those that wear
Whole-souled honesty printed there.

ELLEN PALMER ALLERTON

I am eternally grateful to my mother for many things, but one of the most enduring blessings she brought into my life was to teach me the Catechism at the age of ten that "God is a Spirit, infinite, eternal, and unchangeable in his being, wisdom, power, holiness, justice, goodness, and truth." That definition of God has been with me all my life, and when a man knows in his heart that God is an infinite, eternal, and unchangeable Spirit, it helps to overcome the temptation to limit Him.

Billy Graham

PEACE WITH GOD

Mother was a Christian who shared her faith daily with her family. At night, by the flickering gaslight, the children would sit around her to hear the Scripture. She made the time of worship a delightfully happy one.

F. W. Boreham

The most important thing in Mother's life was her missionary call. This gave her faith to believe for God's keeping power to raise three children in what was known in that era as "the white man's graveyard" of West Africa. (One child almost died of black water fever at the age of two.) It gave her faith to believe for healing and keeping of her good eye (one was lost at the age of five) when African pink eye repeatedly attacked her good one. This kept her going when after forty years of marriage Dad dropped dead of a heart attack while they were preparing to return to Africa. After a short period of mourning she returned to Africa and ministered for another five years before retiring. Thank you, Mother, for showing us how to appropriate God's provision for everyday living.

PEGGY L.

So Long as There Are Homes

. . . So long as there are homes where fires burn
And there is bread;
So long as there are homes where lamps are lit
And prayers are said;
Although people falter through the dark—
And nations grope—
With God himself back of these little homes—
We have sure hope.

GRACE NOLL CROWELL

My mother was the source from which I derived
the guiding principles of my life.

JOHN WESLEY

The mother's heart is the child's school-room.

HENRY WARD BEECHER

Russian Mothers Kept the Lutheran Church Alive

Fifty years ago, Joseph Stalin decided to destroy the Lutheran church in Russia. The Lutherans were to be a case study in how all the Christian denominations might eventually be liquidated.

First, Stalin had the pastors killed or imprisoned. Then the church buildings were confiscated. Bibles, hymnbooks, and religious writings were destroyed. Lutheran families were broken up. Men were forced into the army. Women and children were loaded into boxcars like cattle and scattered throughout the remote regions of the Soviet Union—some to the deserts of the Islamic republics, others to the arctic wastelands of Siberia. In a shockingly brief time, the Lutheran Church of the Soviet Union was wiped off the face of the earth.

But that's not the end of the story. Not by any means.

Though scattered, the Lutheran women worked stubbornly, painfully, to keep their church alive. They had no pastors, no church buildings, no Bibles or hymnbooks. But that didn't stop them. They sought each other out across miles of desolate countryside. They met in one another's homes to pray and minister to each other. They wrote down all the religious instruction they had learned by heart: Bible verses, Luther's catechism, hymns, liturgies. They held religious services. And, at the risk of imprisonment, they passed on the faith to their children.

Over time, some of the husbands managed to rejoin their families. Some of the surrounding people converted. A community of believers was formed. . . . The Lutheran church was reborn. . . . It now meets in more than five hundred house churches. . . . The church has outlasted Communism.

Charles Colson
A DANCE WITH DECEPTION

*I*f I knocked on my mother's door, she always answered;
and if I entered [her writing room] . . . , she never seemed to mind. She
would put down her pen immediately and smile gently and ask what
I wanted. . . . As she turned toward the doorway, with the light from
the window on her face, I could tell she was very glad to see me.

Reeve Lindbergh

(DAUGHTER OF ANNE MORROW LINDBERGH)

Mother was my first Christian influence. From her I experienced unconditional love throughout my life until her death. She loved the Lord and had a servant's heart. She instilled Christian principles into my life with "do unto others" as one of her major themes. She was truly my very best friend.

I am secure in the fact that I have no doubt about where my mother is now, and I know that her self-esteem was raised because the ground at the foot of the cross is level. How thankful I am that a gracious God took the clay of my mother's life and molded a vessel of beauty that brought honor and glory to His name.

MARSHA C.

Youth fades, love droops,
the leaves of friendship fall;
A mother's secret hope
outlives them all.

OLIVER WENDALL HOLMES

The heart of a mother is a deep abyss at the bottom
of which you will always discover forgiveness.

HONORE DE BALZAC

In all the little daily patterns of the home—the laundry going into the same hamper, the sweaters into the same drawer, the hair getting washed and the shoes polished on Saturday nights—God is at work. He delights to glorify Himself in the commonplace. . . . He makes our little daily chores channels of His grace.

ANNE ORTLUND

The great doing of little things makes the great life.

EUGENIA PRICE

Mother had ambitions for all of her children. She and Father both wanted for us as much education as each child was capable of acquiring. Mother inculcated in all of her children a sense of confidence, pride, and ambition. She believed we could do anything. No allowance was made for failure. . . .

And it was Mother who set before us the ideal of service to God, country, and mankind. To spend one's life in the service of others was for Mother the supreme way of life.

Edward L. R. Elson

(pastor for 27 years of the National Presbyterian Church in Washington D. C.)

WIDE WAS HIS PARISH

"*Mother Schmidt washed and ironed busily all day in her shed, cooked the soup over her gypsy fire, and when the daily work was done sat in the shadow of the old omnibus with her children around her, a grateful and contented woman. If anyone asked her what she would do when our bitter winter came, the smile on her face grew graver, but did not vanish, as she laid her worn hands together and answered, with simple faith,—'The good Gott who gave us this home and raised up these friends will not forget us, for He has such as we in His especial charge.'*"

LOUISA MAY ALCOTT
"THE AUTOBIOGRAPHY OF AN OMNIBUS"

My Mother

Who fed me from her gentle breast
And hushed me in her arms to rest,
And on my cheek sweet kisses prest?
My mother.

Who taught my infant lips to pray,
To love God's holy word and day,
And walk in wisdom's pleasant way?
My mother.

And can I ever cease to be
Affectionate and kind to thee
Who wast so very kind to me,—
My mother.

Oh no, the thought I cannot bear;
And if God please my life to spare
I hope I shall reward thy care,
My mother. . . .

Jane Taylor
1783-1824

Dear Mom,

I have never met another who is as giving as you. It seems your whole life is giving your all to anyone who is willing to receive. Now that I have become a mother myself, I look back at the way you took care of all of us—boy do I have a lot to live up to! I hope as I am raising my own children that you will be there to give me advice. I want to do everything I can to give my children the love and understanding you have given to me. You will never know what an impact you have made on my life. I really hope I can be a mom like you.

Love,

PAMELA MEARS

She opens her mouth with wisdom, and on
her tongue is the law of kindness.

PROVERBS 31:26

When my mother sat me down to help me get perspective on
Debbie's death, she did not give me an involved spiritual argument.
Instead, she painted a picture of a little girl bringing home flowers, a
most familiar scene, and of God picking a flower for His garden. . . .
I could see and understand the implication of that picture. It
made sense to me and restored my faith in a loving God.

DALE EVANS ROGERS
IN THE HANDS OF THE POTTER

_M_y mother had often talked to me about the Lord Jesus, and often, as I sat on her knee, with her arms about me she sang, "Jesus the Very Thought of Thee."

Amy Carmichael

Mothers, You Are Great!

I know of no more permanent imprint on a life than the one made by mothers. I guess that's why Mother's Day always leaves me a little nostalgic. Not simply because my mother has gone on (and heaven's probably cleaner because of it!), but because that's the one day the real heroines of our world get the credit they deserve. Hats off to every one of you!

More than any statesman or teacher, more than any minister or physician, more than any film star, athlete, business person, author, scientist, civic leader, entertainer, or military hero . . . you are the most influential person in your child's life.

Never doubt that fact!

Not even when the dishes in the sink resemble the Leaning Tower . . . or the washing machine gets choked and dies . . . or the place looks a wreck and nobody at home stops to say, "Thanks Mom. You're great."

It's still worth it. You are great. This is your time to make the most significant contribution in all of life. Don't sell it short. In only a few years it will all be a memory. Make it a good one.

CHARLES SWINDOLL
THE FINISHING TOUCH

What a gorgeous gift—the gift of birth—placed within the realm of woman's possibilities. Think of it. Bach's mother gave him the gift of birth. Luther's mother gave him the gift of birth. Michelangelo's mother gave him the gift of birth. Beethoven's mother gave him the gift of birth. . . . Without the conscious choice to make this often costly gift of birth . . . the gifts individual people have brought into the stream of history could not have been given.

Edith Schaeffer

(*The Tribute*, by Dennis Rainey)

Dear Mom,

*D*o you remember July 19, 1960? I sure don't, thank the Lord! I'm sure it was traumatic enough for one of us, let alone both of us having to go through it! Although I don't remember the day, I know it was extremely special, because that is the day the Lord delivered me into your arms. Your loving, caring, gentle arms. He knew what a unique woman you were going to be, and that's why He gave you to me. . . .

You are a woman of strength and devotion. Your determination is a beautiful gift from the Lord. Your perseverance, tolerance, patience, honesty, integrity, and ethics are not to be surpassed. Words like **kind, thoughtful, caring,** and **gentle** were created to describe you. . . .

Like God, you gave us a free will to live our lives the way we choose. But unlike so many parents, you gave us a solid foundation based on your attributes that has affected us tremendously, and I thank you from the bottom of my heart for teaching us well.

Thank you for being Mom in labor on July 19, 1960. I never would have known the depths that love could go to had it been someone else.

Love,

DAWN CRANE

*M*others really have their own secret club. Hearts
that understand each other. Common threads
that bind us together in love.

ANN KIEMEL ANDERSON

TEA WITH MOTHER

*F*or at least two centuries, "Come for tea" has been just another way of saying, "Come, let's share a bit of our lives together."

Tea nurtures friendship by inviting us to be present to one another— right now, in the moment. . . . The tea ritual feels safe, comforting, inviting.

Quietly and without threat, it calls us out of ourselves and into relationship. . . . And when we offer tea to someone, we are also offering ourselves. We are saying, "For the next few minutes I will listen to you. I will treat you with respect. I will be present for you."

A TEATIME BLESSING

*L*ord, grant that our time together be steeped in serenity, sweetened by sharing, and surrounded by the warm fragrance of your love.

Amen

EMILIE BARNES

IF TEACUPS COULD TALK

A kind face is a beautiful face.

ANONYMOUS

What a treat to have tea with Mother. Along with a pot of steaming tea, cream, and sugar, serve these wonderfully fluffy biscuits (scones) piping hot from the oven. Smother in butter and top with fresh strawberry preserves and whipped cream. Of course you will want to serve it all in your best china on starched white linen with a lovely bouquet of flowers or some forced winter blossoms.

BUTTERMILK BISCUITS (Scones)

3 cups sifted flour
1 teaspoon salt
1 1/2 teaspoons baking soda
1 teaspoon cream of tartar

2/3 cup shortening
1 1/4 cups buttermilk

Preheat the oven to 450 F.°

Sift the dry ingredients into a bowl. Add the shortening and blend together with a pastry cutter until the mixture resembles cornmeal. Add the buttermilk and stir well.

Place the dough mixture on a lightly floured work surface. Knead the dough lightly just for a minute, being careful not to add too much flour. Roll out to 1/2 inch thickness. Cut the dough into 3-4 inch circles close to each other. Place the circles 1/2 inch apart on a sturdy baking sheet and bake in a preheated 450° oven for 13 minutes.

This recipe yields one dozen large, scrumptious biscuits (scones).

A Tribute to Cleo Lounsberry from Her Daughters

Dear Mom,

When summers at grandmother's came, I'd beg her to take me to visit my aunt, because my aunt resembled you. I'd crawl up in her lap and hug her close and for a time be reminded of you. For a moment, the homesickness would depart, and I'd be ready to resume summer apart from you.

In countless expressions, you exemplified love. But it wasn't until I watched you lay down your life to care for your mother—small and withered and no longer able to move or speak—that I realized how far I had yet to go in the loving. It was as if God Himself had been whispering in your ear how to do it.

I remain amazed at how you make this "loving" thing seem so natural . . . and it often isn't . . . and so easy . . . and it rarely is that. You are the sum, Mother, of the act of loving. And so I continue to watch you. And listen. And learn. . . .

ALYSE L.

My mother impressed me most with her beautiful soprano voice and her love of music. I remember the nights filled with music, when my mother would play the piano or organ and we would gather around to call our favorite songs. Our voices would rise in perfect harmony (or so it seemed to me). While everything outside our home was not harmonious, at times like these we were in cadence.

The first time my own daughter asked me to "sing her favorite song again," it took me back suddenly to the time of my childhood. Glancing down, I saw the look in my daughter's eyes. A look of joy, of wonderment, almost of awe. I saw in her eyes, my own eyes, gazing at my mother when she would sing. What a wonderful gift to pass on to a child.

CAMALA N.

$\mathcal{F}$amily resemblances are inescapable, as much a part of family life as, say, that recipe for vegetable soup and a tendency to weep noisily at sad movies, or the inevitability of glasses in the fifth grade. With an eye cocked for the gesture, the giggle, the blue eyes or the long feet, we tie up our tribe. What every family is confirming, of course, is continuity, and its own sense of self, the things that make the family circle a circle indeed.

SUNDAY HENDRICKSON

*Thou art thy mother's glass,
and she in thee
calls back the lovely April
of her prime.*

WILLIAM SHAKESPEARE

I understood . . . the value of having a mother who had not stopped taking chances and looking at life with delight. It was comforting to know that I was not at the head of the parade, that there was an older, wiser woman moving in front of me.

PHYLLIS THEROUX

Next to God we are indebted to women, first for life itself, and then for making it worth having.

BOVÉE

Mother is my best friend. She has been front and center in my life every step of the way. When I was a young girl, she was there to urge me to do my best. . . . And when the little scrapes and defeats of childhood occurred, Mother was there to turn my sorrows into smiles. . . .

One of the most vivid memories I have of her is on her knees, praying for me, others, and the needs of the world. When I go home to visit, I sleep in the same room with her because we love to talk to each other until we fall asleep.

Mother is unselfish, constantly thinking of others. She endears herself to people because she genuinely cares about every person who crosses her path.

Elizabeth Dole

(TODAY'S CHRISTIAN WOMAN, JULY-AUGUST 1993)

*There is no love on earth, I think,
as potent and enduring as a
mother's love for her child.*

ANN KIEMEL
ANDERSON

I associate childhood prayers with bedtime and warm milk, with a turned-down lamp or flickering candle, and with the reassuring presence of my mother as we faced the adventure of another night. The routine of prayer was snuggled somewhere between the protests or the tired acceptance of bed, and the giggles and squabbles that would follow until sleep came.

David A. C. Read

(pastor for many years of Madison Avenue Presbyterian Church in New York City)

THIS GRACE GIVEN

No nation ever had a better friend than the mother who taught her children to pray.

ANONYMOUS

My mother always gave the fireplace and hearth a fresh whitewashing the day before Christmas, and washed, starched, and ironed the white lace curtains. . . .

We all dressed in our Sunday dresses for Christmas dinner. . . . My mother would have been in the kitchen since five o'clock and half the night as well, and when the dinner was ready we would gather around the table and sit for hours enjoying all the things she had prepared.

EDNA LEWIS

THE TASTE OF COUNTRY COOKING

"*When Peter got home his mother forgave him, because she was so glad to see that he had found his shoes and coat. Cotton-tail and Peter folded up the pocket-handkerchief, and old Mrs. Rabbit strung up the onions and hung them from the kitchen ceiling, with the bunches of herbs.*"

BEATRIX POTTER
"THE TALE OF BENJAMIN BUNNY"

A Tribute to Edith Gibbs from Her Six Children

As a girl you helped your parents make
their prairie farm a home.

As a teenager you left that home to work
alone in the city and attend high school.

As a young woman you became one of the few women
of your time to earn a college degree.

As a wife you made the parsonage a cosy haven,
living a life of loving sacrifice.

As a widow you overcame your grief to raise six children alone,
teaching English at high school and love at home.

As a grandmother you never forget a birthday
or miss an opportunity to pray.

We thank you, Mom, for your godly example of motherhood—
it is our invaluable legacy and that of our children and their children.

We love you Mom,

JIM, DAVID, MARYLEE, CARL, BILL, AND GWEN

From an early age, my shelves were bursting with
books about every subject imaginable. My mother
spent hours reading aloud to her children.

Franky Schaeffer

*M*y mother taught me to memorize great passages of the Bible.
Text after text, passage after passage . . . were stored away in the memory
and became part of the daily thinking . . . and have continued
a precious treasure all down through the years.

Bishop James Cannon, Jr.

My Mom, Too!

*Y*ou raised them well, loving and kind
and to great amazement God made one mine.
He knew He could create and mold godly men through you,
and in knowing you'd do a fine job, He gave you two!

But the Lord took you even further, though you're unaware,
and gave you extra love for me that you're always glad to share.
You're a true example of how he wants us to stand—firm and tall,
and that is why I call you my *mom*, not my mother-in-law.

Thank you Mom for being who God intended you to be,
and thank you Lord for giving her especially to me.

KELLY S.

*D*oes a child that lies in the arms of its mother need to fear,
surrounded by her providing love which long before has thought of
everything that is good and necessary for it? No, certainly not.

KARL BARTH

There is a place in most mothers' hearts that seeks to protect children from harm and evil and unfairness. For most women . . . it is as natural as breathing and sleeping.

ANN KIEMEL ANDERSON

$\mathcal{M}$other—that was the bank where we
deposited all our hurts and worries.

T. DEWITT TALMAGE

Mother's Prima Ballerina

In my memory, my childhood years form a mellow hodgepodge of love, joy, and the thrill of conquering new challenges. I was definitely a tomboy, but somehow my mother persuaded me to take ballet lessons, and I've always been grateful for that. The teacher was a woman from Russia who had moved to the area for some reason, and she was a very strict, very disciplined instructor. She taught lessons once a week in the American Legion Hall, and her mother would come along to play the piano for us while we danced. My mother sewed all my costumes for the recitals, of course—elaborate sequined-and-feathered outfits that seem just as enchanting today in the old photographs as they did so many years ago. After the Russian teacher moved away, Mom drove me to Angelton, a town about twenty miles away, so I could continue dance lessons with Ruth and Sara Munson, two sisters from West Columbia.

Ruth Ryan

(wife of Nolan Ryan)

COVERING HOME

A Potpourri for Mother

To a basin of dried scented roses add a
handful of dried knotted Marjoram, lemon
thyme, Rosemary, Lavender flowers all
well dried, the rind of one lemon and one
orange dried to powder, six dried bay leaves,
half an ounce of bruised cloves, a teaspoon
of Allspice. Mix well together and stir occasionally.

Dated 1895

BY ANY OTHER NAME

A Mother's Birthday

Lord Jesus, Thou has known
A mother's love and tender care:
And thou wilt hear,
While for my own
Mother most dear
I make this birthday prayer.

Protect her life, I pray,
who gave the gift of life to me;
And may she know,
From day to day,
The deepening glow
of joy that comes from Thee. . . .

Ah, hold her by the hand,
As once her hand held mine;
And though she may
Not understand
Life's winding way,
Lead her in peace divine.

I cannot pay my debt
For all the love that she has given;
But Thou, love's Lord,
Wilt not forget
Her due reward,—
Bless her in earth and heaven.

HENRY VAN DYKE

1852-1933

A Tribute to My Mom, Jeannine Sawyer of Brownwood, Texas

As a single mom in the '50s, with three young children and no education, my mom faced many challenges. She worked long, hard hours in a non-air-conditioned woolen mill for little pay. The amazing thing was her optimistic attitude. I remember how excited she was when she was able to get us a place to live in a government-subsidized housing project. It was cheap, but it was clean.

At first we had very little furniture, not even a table for the kitchen. This didn't bother Mom. For our first meal, she fixed us hot dogs, and we sat on the floor on a blanket. She said, "Isn't this great! We're having a picnic in our very own kitchen." She made the situation seem like fun. We laughed and joked and had a great time. Much later I realized what a true marvel she was. Instead of feeling down and beleaguered, she embraced the good in life and taught us to do the same. How grateful I am for the example she set.

KAREN G.

A true mother is not merely a provider, housekeeper, comforter, or companion. A true mother is primarily and essentially a trainer.

Ruth Bell Graham

$\mathcal{T}$he home is to be a center of service, a base for acts of charity and kindness, a place where love for neighbor becomes a way of life.

David A. Hubbard

It's difficult to know what counts in this world. Most of us count credits, honor, dollars. But at the bulging center of mid-life, I am beginning to see that the things that really matter take place not in the boardrooms, but in the kitchens of the world. Memory, imagination, love are some of those things. Service to God and the ones we love is another.

GARY ALLEN SLEDGE

(READER'S DIGEST, SEPTEMBER 1989)

The apples were stored in the basement because it was much cooler there. Grandma would send her youngest, my mom, down to carry them up for the family with the instructions, "Bring me the apples that are starting to go bad, and we'll eat those first." Now that's a great way to make use of every apple in the basket, but what is the result? You're always eating half-rotten apples! When could you enjoy the fresh, sweet, succulent fruit?

From that experience my mom determined that she would always give her family and friends the best of whatever she had. It was her way of showing how important we were to her. If the fresh baked cake was sitting on the counter awaiting guests or the church social and we wanted a bite, it was ours for the asking. She would cut a piece right out of the middle for us, slice up the rest into squares, and place them on a separate dish. No one was the wiser.

My mom is a true servant and woman of God. She not only gives the best of whatever she has, but she gives of herself—in time, love, and energy. She teaches by example the principle of being a channel for God.

Thanks Mom for the good apples, the first piece of cake, and a life-long example of giving.

DEBBIE W.

Still Praying for You, Son

As I shoved the last volume in place, my eyes fell upon an old work by a British pastor of yesteryear, F. B. Meyer. . . . It was not his words that spoke to me that evening, however, but the words of my mother. For as I began looking through it, I realized the book had once been a part of her library; after her death in 1971 it had found its way into mine. Little did she realize that her words would become part of her legacy to me. In her inimitable handwriting, my mother had added her own observations, prayers, and related Scriptures in the margins throughout the book. Inside the back cover she had written: "Finishing reading this, May 8, 1958."

When I saw that date . . . 1958 . . . memory carried me back to a tiny island in the South Pacific where I had spent many lonely months as a Marine. There, in May of '58 I had reached a crossroad in my own spiritual pilgrimage. In fact, I had entered these words in my own journal at the time: "The Lord has convinced me that I am to be in His service. I need to begin my plans to prepare for a lifetime of ministry."

Amazingly, it was the same month of that same year that my mother had finished Meyer's book. As I scanned her words, I found one reference after another to her prayers for me as I was far, far away . . . her concern for my spiritual welfare . . . her desire for God's best in my life.

And in that moment I thanked God anew for the touch of my mother's love and the effectiveness of her prayers. I bowed my head and wept with gratitude. . . .

In the gathering dusk I smiled and said softly, "Thank you, Mother." I could almost hear her voice answering, "Charles, I love you. I'm still praying for you, Son. Keep walking with God. Finish strong!"

Charles Swindoll
THE FINISHING TOUCH

Ah, my child, while I was yet a little boy, while I yet
sat upon my mother's knee, I believed in God the Father,
who rules up there in heaven, good and great.

HEINRICH HEINE

She makes coffee in the mornings, gets her children off to school, and tries to make ends meet at the market. She is very bright, her snapping eyes tell me. Yet she serves. She manages here in this restaurant. She is capable of more.

That is something women everywhere share in common. Perhaps that is why they can make do, be happy wherever they are; they're used to making contentment out of whatever comes—always making something from nothing, stretching the stew, remaking the worn-out clothes or opportunity into something "new" and presentable, smiling and caressing in spite of their own inclinations to tears and fatigue—mothering the world.

Gloria Gaither

WE HAVE THIS MOMENT

Recently I was called home. My Dad lay in the hospital in critical condition. Within hours of my arrival, he was placed in ICU. After visiting hours at the hospital were over, my mother and I returned home. As I drove, I noticed how tired Mother appeared and how worried. She wasn't very talkative, but she began to hum an old hymn to herself. Mother has always been a "hummer." Whether she was working around the house, shopping, driving to an appointment— she always hummed a song. As we drove that day, I suddenly realized the secret of her happy disposition and her ability to remain at peace in any situation. She hums! Since then, when I find myself afraid of the circumstances of life or when things seems out of control, I smile, think of a song, and begin to hum.

NANCY L. S.

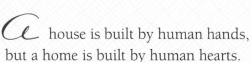

A house is built by human hands,
but a home is built by human hearts.

ANONYMOUS

It is from God that parents receive their children,
and it is to God that they should lead them.

DIETRICH BONHOEFFER

> *I learned more about Christianity from my mother than from all the theologians of England.*
>
> JOHN WESLEY

"Mom, I can still remember coming home from school to the smell of homemade cookies. As I sat down to snack on a warm snickerdoodle, I probably thought, 'Everybody does this—everybody's got a mom at home who's able to make cookies for her kids, who's always there when her son needs her, and who's able to give him an example of self-sacrifice.'"

JOHN HAILEY
THE TRIBUTE, BY DENNIS RAINEY

When I was a young man, I had plenty of people to wipe away my tears. I had two big sisters who put me under their wings. I had a dozen or so aunts and uncles. I had a mother who worked nights as a nurse and days as a mother—excercising both professions with tenderness. . . .

My mother still lives in the same house. You couldn't pay her to move. The house that seemed so big when I was a boy now feels tiny. On the wall are pictures of Mom in her youth—her hair autumn-brown, her face irresistibly beautiful. I see her now —still healthy, still vivacious, but with wrinkles, graying hair, slower step. Would that I could wave the wand and make everything new again. Would that I could put her once again in the strong embrace of the high-plains cowboy she loved and buried. Would that I could stretch out the wrinkles and take off the bifocals and restore the spring to her step, would that I could make everything new. . . but I can't.

Max Lucado
THE APPLAUSE OF HEAVEN

*W*omen are aristocrats, and it is always the mother who makes us feel that we belong to the better sort.

JOHN LANCASTER SPALDING

Mother Prepares for Revival Sunday

Although I didn't think about it at the time, I wonder how my mother made it each year to Revival Sunday, with so much to do and without ever varying from the calm and quiet manner that was her nature. Until the field work, which she loved, was over, she had no time to begin her own important preparations for Revival Week. And so, during the week leading up to second Sunday, as well as doing her regular household chores and caring for her brood of chickens, guinea hens, turkeys, and ducks, and her own vegetable garden, she would cut out and sew new dresses of white muslin for the six of us and our two adopted cousins as well as for herself, usually finishing the last button-holes and sashes late Saturday night in between the cooking that she would have begun for the next days' noontime dinner at the church. . . .

My mother never started her cooking until late on the eve of Revival Sunday. By this time she would have everything gathered in and laid out that she would need, and, I guess, a carefully planned schedule laid out in her mind as well. When we were bathed and turned into bed, no pies or cakes had yet been made. But when we came hurrying down on Sunday morning, the long, rectangular dining-room table would be covered with cakes ready to be iced and pie dishes lined with pastry dough to be filled and baked.

Edna Lewis
THE TASTE OF COUNTRY COOKING

My mother was a wonderful role model . . . a woman of prayer and the Word. If I stayed up late to study for an exam and went downstairs to speak to Mother, I'd find her on her knees in prayer. Early in the morning she'd be sitting at her desk reading her Bible. And during the day, if she had a few minutes, she'd slip back to her desk again.

Mother taught me by her example that there's nothing more satisfying than a personal love relationship with the Lord. It's what made her strong. When Daddy would come home exhausted from ministry, my mother's unflagging faith consistently encouraged him. I'm convinced that without a Ruth Graham, there would never have been the Billy Graham the world has come to know. Her role of ministry to our family was tremendously important then . . . and now.

Anne Graham Lotz

TODAY'S CHRISTIAN WOMAN, AUGUST 1996

House and Home

A house is built of logs and stone,
of tiles and posts and piers;
A home is built of loving deeds
That stand a thousand years.

VICTOR HUGO

"*Every mother practices the ritual of counting tiny fingers
and toes, cupping the small head in one's hand, stroking gossamer
hair, and trying to determine just whose side of the family is
responsible for those ears and that nose—all rites of
new motherhood, both private and public, that
mark the beginning of a whole new world.*"

PAMELA SCURRY
CRADLE AND ALL

𝒢racias Madre por darme muy buenos principios y valores.
Gracias por enseñarme a respetar al projimo, pero mas
que todo, Madre, gracias por tu amor y cariño.

(Thank you Mom for giving me very good principles and values.
Thank you for teaching me to respect and be kind to others, but most
of all, Mom, thanks for your kindness and love.)

RAY J. LLEVERINO

Ray declares that his mother makes the most delicious enchiladas in Texas. Here is her recipe (translated, of course). The recipe will serve 4 adults—unless they are hungry sons, and then it will serve 2.

Enchiladas Verdes Suizas

1 1/2 –2 cups cooked chicken breasts, shredded
salt • pepper

1 dozen white corn tortillas
(homemade are the best if you can find them)
1–1 1/2 cups of sour cream
1 can of green salsa
(1/4 cup for mild, 1/2 cup for spicy)
1 1/2–2 cups of Asadero cheese, shredded
(Monterey Jack cheese is a good substitute)
cooking oil

Season shredded chicken to taste with salt and pepper.

Soften each of the tortillas by dipping briefly in about 1/4 inch of hot cooking oil. Be careful not to leave the tortillas in the oil too long or they will become crisp. Drain the softened tortillas on paper towels. Place a little bit of shredded chicken and some of the shredded cheese in the center of each tortilla. Roll the tortilla around the filling and place in a lightly greased baking dish, seam side down. Sprinkle a little of the remaining cheese over the rolled tortillas. (Reserve some cheese.)

In the remaining oil in the skillet heat the green salsa until it begins to bubble. Stir in the sour cream. (If the sauce seems too spicy for your taste add a bit more sour cream.) Pour the heated mixture over the tortillas and top with the remaining shredded cheese. (Add more cheese if you like.)

Cover the dish and bake at 350F° for 20 minutes. Serve bubbling hot!

¡Riquizimas!

*I have been told
that my mother,
when she surmised
from the face of
the physician that
her life and that
of her child could
not both be saved,
begged him to
spare the child. . . .
So through
these many years
of mine, I have
seldom thanked
God for His
mercies without
thanking Him
for my mother.*

JAMES M.
LUDLOW

1919

Three Cheers for Mother!

Over the centuries she's worked as hard as
father and for very different reasons.

He has built the houses; she's added the colors, the smells, the music.

He has shaped constitutions to make citizens protected;
she has sewn flags to make them weep and cheer.

He has mustered armies and police forces to put down oppression;
she has prayed for them and patted them on the back
and sent them off with their heads up.

He has shaped decisions; she has added morale.

Celebrate the mother! She, too, no less than the father, has,
under God, shaped a magnificent human tradition.

ANNE ORTLUND
DISCIPLINES OF THE HOME

My Altar

. . . The things in life that are worthy
Were born in my mother's breast
And breathed into mine by the magic
Of the love her life expressed.
The years that have brought me to manhood
Have taken her far from me;
But memory keeps me from straying
Too far from my mother's knee.

JOHN H. STYLES, JR.

A mother's arms are made
of tenderness, and children sleep
soundly in them.

VICTOR HUGO

I still remember vividly the desperate, empty feeling I had in third grade on that one and only time when I came home after school to face a locked front door. My mother wasn't home! It had never happened before. There I stood paralyzed with fear, alone and crying.

Fortunately my despair was brief; Mom drove up in just a few minutes. Her welcome hug flooded over me and I felt secure again. All was well in my world. Today I'm thankful that my mom's hug still brings warmth and relief. Moms are good at that!

LYNN R.

A s for me and my house, we will serve the LORD.

JOSHUA 24:15

A husband and a wife dare a great deal when they bring a child into the world. . . . It is a risk to share with God in the creation of a human soul, but it is one that is well worth taking. Such an adventure may help us to know one of the deepest and sweetest secrets of human blessedness.

Clovis Chappell

Mother's Day Cards

This poem was found on a handmade mother's day card tucked inside a musty, old book in a quaint antique shoppe:

Dear Mother,

I love you
For the part of me
That you bring out;
I love you
For putting your hand
Into my heaped-up heart
And passing over
All the foolish, weak things
That you can't help
Dimly seeing there,
And for drawing out
Into the light
All the beautiful belongings
That no one else had looked'
Quite far enough to find. . . .

I do love you mother.

Your adoring daughter,

Mary Marcée

$\mathcal{B}$engy had made his [Mother's Day] card himself
by cutting letters out of the newspaper. . . .
Roses are red
Violets are blue;
My Mom's the best
And she's pretty too.

On the back was this postscript:

P.S. I have a surprise for you.
Love Benjy

I was happy. I had a very creative son, and I was probably the only
mother in America who got a live largemouth bass for Mother's Day!

GLORIA GAITHER
WE HAVE THIS MOMENT

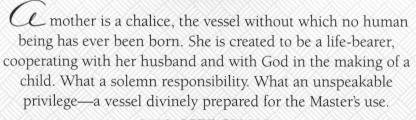

a mother is a chalice, the vessel without which no human being has ever been born. She is created to be a life-bearer, cooperating with her husband and with God in the making of a child. What a solemn responsibility. What an unspeakable privilege—a vessel divinely prepared for the Master's use.

ELISABETH ELLIOT

A Simple Moment of Remembrance

On my mother's birthday last year, I thought about her and how special she had been to me. On impulse, I pushed back from the breakfast table, found a small birthday candle in the cabinet, stuck it into my boiled egg, lighted it, turned off the kitchen lights, and with lifted coffee cup I sang, ". . . happy birthday, dear Mother, happy birthday to you." Maybe that sounds weird. Admittedly, it is out of the ordinary—but I'm glad, because my mother, too, was out of the ordinary. Those few moments spent for her, on her birthday, reminded me again of the values she instilled in me for life. Much of what I am today I owe to her. I am the product of her love and devotion to praying for me, her encouragement, her emphasis on the arts and upon spiritual training. That simple moment of remembrance . . . provided enrichment and gratitude throughout my whole day as I thought back on those wonderful memories I relived that morning.

Luci Swindoll

YOU BRING THE CONFETTI: GOD BRINGS THE JOY

As long as we lived in Philadelphia, we actually walked all the way home for lunch every day. We liked to. When we burst in the door there was Mother, and there was the hot soup. It was nice to smell the soup, and it was nice that Mother was always there for us. Always.

ELISABETH ELLIOT

THE SHAPING OF A CHRISTIAN FAMILY

And a servant of the Lord must not quarrel but must be kind to everyone, a good teacher, and patient.

2 TIMOTHY 2:24

I am blessed with a mother who is a true servant of the Lord. Her kindness to every unique individual she comes in contact with has made her a dear friend of many, including her children. I have often heard friends remark with amazement at her years of working with mentally and physically handicapped children. But what has been even more amazing to me is her quickness to forgive and her encouragement for those whose helpless situations are of their own choosing. Her instant willingness to reach out to these hurting souls gives them the glimpse of God's love that renews their desire to fight again the battles of this world. Her loving acceptance is a constant example of the Lord's desire for each of us to be more gracious and longsuffering.

LARA L.

Dear Mom,

I can still smell the freshly baked cookies and taste the big glass of cold milk that were always on the table waiting for me when I arrived home from a busy day at school. You were synonymous with June Cleaver on "Leave It to Beaver." You were always home when I got there. You made sure I had a fresh scrubbed look at all times, glistening hair, and a starched dress. You saw to it that I had music lessons the first twenty years of my life, which taught me great self-discipline.

I look at you now with advanced Alzheimer's disease and realize you are gone. Once in a great while a spark of how you were in the past glows; your dry sense of humor breaks through the barrier, and it is amazing how you can still pray and talk about heavenly things. You are not my mother any longer but only the outer shell of what once was. My hope for you is that somewhere in your mind once in a while circuits connect and you, if only for a second, realize that you are loved.

MARCI I.

To love and be loved is to feel the sun from both sides.

Barbara Johnson

MOMMIE N' ME COOKIES

1 cup butter (softened slightly) • **3 tablespoons sugar**
2 cups flour • **1 teaspoon vanilla**
1/2 cup nuts ground fine • **powdered sugar**

Preheat oven to 400 F°.

Mix all ingredients and shape into half-moon shapes. Place on ungreased baking sheets. Bake for 8 to 10 minutes. Remove from baking sheets and roll in powdered sugar while still warm. Set on cookie racks to cool briefly.

Enjoy with a glass of cold milk or a cup of hot tea. Yum!

My mother is so precious to me—because I know how hard it was for her to be pregnant with me. I think I was the worst pregnancy she ever had. I really think she is great for being pregnant with me for nine whole months!

My mother is so precious to me—because when I was about to die with asthma in the hospital she stayed by my side. I'm so thankful that she was there to care for me.

My mother is so precious to me—because she is a strong woman who loves God and because she seeks His will and does it. She teaches my sisters and me God's ways. She is like a flower because she is so sweet. I learn something new about her every day.

She loves me and cares for me, and although she is not perfect, I love her.

LYNETTE A. (12 YEARS OLD)

I love old mothers—mothers with white hair,
and kindly eyes, and lips grown softly sweet with
murmured blessings over sleeping babes.

CHARLES S. ROSS

I cannot think of my Mom without thinking of the beautiful way she cares about others, her giving of self, and her concern for everyone around her. When she was going in for open-heart surgery, she was an inspiration to everyone around her.

I smile when I think of the last few minutes before she was wheeled to the operating room, a scenario so typical of Mom. My dad's boss had sent her a lovely vase of red roses that were delivered to her at the hospital that morning before the operation. While she appreciated this thoughtfulness, she also realized that she would be in ICU for some time and did not want the roses to go to waste. Just before the nurses came to wheel her to the operating room, she took her roses and went down the hall stepping into each room and giving a red rose to every patient on the floor so that each one could enjoy her flowers and have something beautiful to brighten the room. The man with the gurney was literally chasing her down the hall trying to find her to take her to surgery. She was telling him, "Just one more room." Even at a time like that, she was giving to others and sharing what was given to her.

PAT B.

I have no greater joy than to hear that my children walk in truth.

3 JOHN 1:4

*M*other always smelled beautiful. I remember burrowing into her neck just for the soft loveliness of scented skin. After smell came sound, the sound of her voice, singing to me, talking. I took the beauty of her voice for granted until I was almost grown up.

Madeleine L'Engle
THE SUMMER OF THE GREAT GRANDMOTHER